A Rag Doll After My Heart

T0311146

A Rag Doll After My Heart

A Poetic Novel

ANURADHA VAIDYA

Translated from the original Marathi by
SHRUTI NARGUNDKAR

ZUBAAN
128B Shahpur Jat, 1st Floor
NEW DELHI 110 049
Email: contact@zubaanbooks.com
Website: www.zubaanbooks.com

First published by Zubaan Publishers Pvt Ltd 2015

ISBN 978 93 83074 09 9

Zubaan is an independent feminist publishing house based in New Delhi with a strong academic and general list. It was set up as an imprint of India's first feminist publishing house, Kali for Women, and carries forward Kali's tradition of publishing world quality books to high editorial and production standards. *Zubaan* means tongue, voice, language, speech in Hindustani. Zubaan publishes in the areas of the humanities, social sciences, as well as in fiction, general non-fiction, and books for children and young adults under its Young Zubaan imprint.

Typeset in Adobe Devanagari 11/14 by Jojy Phillip, New Delhi 110 015
Printed at Raj Press, R-3 Inderpuri, New Delhi 110 012

Introduction

Maajhi Chindhyanchi Bahuli is a story of the relationship between a mother and daughter who are not linked by blood or birth. The relationship is conceived and cherished not in the mother's womb, but in her heart. It is a tale of how their relationship began and grew in joy, weathered deep trouble and finally triumphed. The pull of parenthood, and the desire to shower affection and love on a child is one of the most instinctive and primal needs. The relationship described here is the result of this compulsive need. Here, a human being is prepared to bestow love and wait patiently to be loved in return. In her early years, the object of affection laps up all the attention she gets, but growing up and coming into knowledge brings on feelings of loss of identity, insecurity and resentment. For the troubled soul in the spoor of its roots, the affection and love that has been so nourishing and life giving can turn into a trap and loved ones can become strangers. The one whose need it is to love is deeply shaken, hurt and feels rejected. While both struggle with the cross currents of conflicting emotions the world outside is re-launches and consolidates its opposition to this relationship. Social criticism, mockery, distrust, condescension and disapproval become the bane of the relationship. The two people most affected by this internal and external maelstrom have to contend not only with their own conflicted feelings, but have also to deal with the battle for a rightful place for it in the world outside. And then, almost as if by divine orchestration, comes the moment of truth that validates this relationship. Slowly but surely the relationship flourishes and reaches newer heights. This is a tale of the path travelled by a mother and a daughter in one such relationship.

Anuradha Vaidya

My Gambit

I come from a family of writers, poets, musicians and literature enthusiasts. My mother encouraged me to read Marathi from a very young age and I grew to love the language – both as a mother tongue and as a medium of literary expression. I read and was greatly influenced by my aunt Anuradha Vaidya's works from an early age. I identified in her writing references to family legends and stories, familiar traits, our family's own brand of humour and that inherited and shared ability to look wryly at even the simplest and quotidian subjects and objects and see beauty, humour and a special significance in them.

Majhi Chindhyanchi Bahuli impressed me the most with the imminent suitability of its form to its theme and content. A perfect fit, the poetic format of this novella supports the very strong overflow of a myriad of emotions interactively engaging the reader in deciphering and creating meaning by joining the dots and quite literally the line ends. It compels readers to linger or jump back and forth across stanzas and lines in their enthusiasm to navigate, interpret, and savour the beauty of the expression, both in the turn of phrase and the coinage of new words. The overarching, almost allegorical imagery of life as a game played on the worldly board by people pawns at the behest of the Master Player was very striking. And although it may not have been quite novel, the sustained use of the imagery in a way that was particularly relevant to the mother's situation so captured my imagination that I had decided, after reading the novel in one go when it was first published, that one day I would attempt to translate it into English.

The urge to write was always latent in me and surfaced every now and then. But when I was really ready to write, I wanted to test and try my ability of wordplay with something close to my heart and home and thus, settled on translating *Majhi Chindhyanchi Bahuli*. I started well, but halfway through had to stash it away for ten long years as another, more prosaic but equally creative enterprise demanded my sole attention. The minute I was able to, I returned to this enjoyable endeavour, this time determined to complete it.

A most challenging and rewarding task this, I immersed myself completely in the poem. I don't know, nor do I worry much, if I have adhered to the principles of translation or whether I have just adapted the poetic novel. I wrote as I read - again and again, finding an apt analogy here and an impossible equivalent there. A semblance of conventions of writing was maintained by the first person narrative and the use of dialogues, but the tenses and verbs found their own wanton ways to express meaning without detraction. Sukanya Prakashan, the publisher of the original work, exhorted critics and readers to accept the unconventional format and the neologisms which only accentuate the beauty of the expression. I have tried these very strategies. Nay, they burst forth spontaneously, most naturally, in this English version too. *Majhi Chindyanchi Bahuli* was lauded by all. It moved many to tears by its depiction of emotions and situations and others to marvel at its sheer beauty as a *kavyambari*, a poetic novel or novel in poetry form. By translating it into *A Rag Doll After My Heart* I hope to bring this beautiful story to a larger audience, to enjoy this heart wrenchingly appealing tale of a mother and daughter conveyed to you in a very unusual but engaging genre.

Anuradha Vaidya wrote with a courageous conviction in her

own ability as a wordsmith to convey this tale – a faith as audacious as that of the protagonist mother who decided to make for herself a rag doll after her own heart.

I thank Anuradha Vaidya for having the same fond faith in me to present her work in English.

I also thank my family for getting and staying as excited as I was about the project over the ten years.

Melbourne

Australia

Shruti Nargundkar

One

When we set the board with pawns
And began the game of life, it dawned on me
It was but a ruse, a pretext, the players
Ostensibly make moves of play, but the
Outcome is predetermined, predestined,
My mind still lingered over the toys
Of my childhood, my kitchen set and the doll's house
But I was warned,
The game of life must be played
The rules decided by fate,
I discovered very early in the game
That once it begins
There is no dealing or turn taking,
We are played, moved back, forth and across
Mouthing dialogues and following directions
Like well-crafted characters on stage
It was no different for me, nor others around me
All of us pawns, moving along preordained sequences
Love, affection, supplication, pity, obsession, joy, regret, thought,
Their roaring, soaring, boasting, leaping,
Sorrow, poverty, suffering and helplessness
Ego, pride, conceit…
All garbed in similar robes
Like cranes, flying in formation.

They reckon, 'we set up the game'
I too set up the game, like everybody else
The game progressed a little and then it was time
To receive gifts, another game this,
A little different, a sweet game
They gave out sweet little dolls
Shiny, chubby, cherubic dolls
Plump, fat, thin and scrawny
Dark, ugly, weak, emaciated, healthy
All kinds of dolls…
The giver giving generously
Takers taking their fill
Coveting, choosing, deciding, selecting from the enormous heap
One, two, occasionally the third
Sometimes a greedy player hankering for more
Raising hands in supplication
The giver losing count
Giving again and again to those who had enough

The crowd, the crushing crowd!
An ant, I crawl my way
Steadfastly to the heap
Only to find they were all gone.
Not a single doll left for me
Satisfaction and smugness among those who received
Disappointment, hope and despair in some
Like me and my mate,
Weakly consoling me while staunching his own dismay.
The game resumed and we joined in again
Some with coffers full, others with empty hands, we began

To play in earnestness, those with dolls
Playing with them, the empty-handed ones trying to sneak a touch
Like a pauper fearfully touching the robes
Of a prince, so rich and fascinating.
I had a game, set for me,
The decisions taken for me
My partner selected for me
But I was not content to follow.

I untied my own bundle of old rags, my very own,
Picked, sorted, chose bits and pieces
Woollen, silken, coarse, soft, even shot with gold
Scissors of determination, needles of pain and threads of affection
My tools to fashion out a beautiful doll, just for me!
Tailor-made for me by me, nobody gave her to me.
I blew life into her breath
And she opened her eyes
I saw flames of my resoluteness in her innocent eyes
Trying to match the rhythm of my heartbeat
To hers, I realized I was no longer without a doll,
Instead, I had my very own.

Two

I bedecked her, and showed her off
Everyone watched, while at the game
Which I too was still playing, this time with my own doll
They scorned her, 'What sort of a doll is this?
So ugly, uncouth, and you say you have fashioned her yourself!
If you were so keen, why didn't you ask us?
Any one of us would have considered giving one away.
A rag doll at that! To be thrown away after play
What did you say? You want to keep her till the end of the game?
Whose game, yours or hers?
They abandon you; you'll be filled with regret
Such bastard dolls, no family, no roots, no antecedents
Throw her away before it's too late!'

Little did they know, I loved my doll!
They pitied me, humoured me
'All right, keep her, play with her; see her to the end of the game
If she lasts, good for you, if she doesn't, it's her fate!'
Some empty ones like me criticised my covetousness
'What He gives is His gift, how can you aspire to match it?'
But others admired my audacity
'You will no longer feel that emptiness,' they said

My tiny, twinkle-eyed innocent little doll!
Blissfully unaware of all this turmoil
Hunger made her lunge for me
I clasped her to my breast
My poor little doll
Suckled on my desert-dry affection.
I soaked my pallav with tears
And my ravenous doll began to nurse
Springs of love flooded my body
My doll revelled, drenched and satiated
I watched her closely
My body and hers
Our blood the same colour, sunrise red.
She is mine, only mine
I have breathed life into her lifeless form
Made her from my life, every fibre of my warp and weft
How is she different?
Why will she leave me?
I am she
And she is me.
We have no existence separate
From one another
We are inextricably entwined together
She is my choice, my daughter
I don't need any favours or charity
Nor the jealous disapproval of those gifted
Don't I know how
They hid their dolls away from my eyes?
I still hurt, my wounds sore from their torches
But my doll will soothe them
Her being will heal my pain.

Three

I spin like a top, wheels on my feet
The game plays on
I have my sweet doll now
But I must slow down
Savour my own feelings, the hunger, the thirst
And hers too
It is she who orients me, she who gives my spinning new meaning
She who makes time fly by on wings of hope
Life flow like the river Ganges
My day breaks for her, my night sets for her
Time belongs to her
I am absorbed in her
And she depends on me.
When we can bear to look away from each other
We traverse the game board
Moving a square ahead, or crossways
Charmed pawns, the two of us
Yet objects of ridicule for others
To each their own, but the rule of the game
Demands decision and judgment
So we are told
But we are like creatures possessed!
We forget all else
The rules, the game, the board
I found paradise in her

She was my paradise, my world
Light of foot and joyful
I rejoiced in bathing her, anointing, dressing her
I had to live it all before endgame
To let in the sweetness and light
Before the doors were shut tight
The game had just begun, who can say when the day
And night will flit away doe-footed
Leaving dreams undreamt?

She, the product of my tenacity
Not a gift, nor gratuity
Crafted by me, my imagination
Thus invaluable; my life.
I want to know her completely
Look at her reflection inside out
With each passing day
Wrapping the warmth of the darkness around us
Embracing my doll, she enters my heart
Her breath in step with mine
I hold her tight
My innocent little doll touches her tiny palm to my eyes
Drawing away my teardrops
Would that I had not wasted so many precious tears
Placed them before her in the hot sands of my misery
Perhaps she would have treasured them
Valued them to find her way into the uncertain future!
I wish to bequeath her my fortune
Ropes of tears, medallions of scars, gems of joy and sorrow
Her priceless heirlooms.

Something like this happens every day
And notches are marked on the scoreboard of play
Tucked into the blanket of darkness, her eyes half-closed
As if to receive the sun's rays at a minute's notice
Her head pillowed on hope and aspiration
When my lullaby touches her through my caresses
Does she dream? Of today? Of tomorrow? Of a future filled with hope?
Or is it my image she sees
At the altar of her closed lids?
Her tired eyelids rest
Her lashes warm against her cheeks

Lips slightly parted in a half-smile
Teasingly dimpling her chubby cheeks
Let me not brush back those lustrous strands
Lest I wake her, make her cry
They say dolls grow in their sleep
Let her grow big and strong
Let her sleep

Will she lose herself in sleep? Will she stray?
The sound of my lullaby travels with her
Leading her by the hand if she loses her way
Bringing her back to me
To fill my life with sunshine, every day.

Four

On another such incandescent morning
On the rooftop terrace with my doll
Watering the roses, stray drops glistening in her curls
My doll so happy
Her face alight with joy
Gurgling and clapping, I lean to pick those pearls
And she runs away, far far away, teasing
Laughing, her rose lips parted
Like a velvet-lined casket opening
Revealing a row of perfect pearls.
Stunned, I stare, an urge to hold and kiss her
Wells up in me, I run to her and she to me
Throwing her arms around me in a satin snare
Delighted she exclaims, 'Mother!'
Mother! A word as sacred as the *Omkar Naad*
Nature's first utterance, primeval, everlasting, eternal
A right easily exercised by even the lowliest life forms
Denied to me so far, but now bestowed
Engraved by her soft hands on my forehead, my fate!
My ordinary craft in making her
Rewarded, raised to the heights of creativity
My seeds never did sprout
But my branches burst out green rays
My lineage had stopped at me, she built
A bridge to the future

A link to posterity, pouring life into
My dried and tired body.

Arid, sterile, loveless, useless.
She scraped away the scum of infamy
And preserved, purified, my spring
Of crystal clear water, now solely for her
I bear her plaque, her presence
Rooting me, defining me, my fence
Encircling me, her milestones fascinating
Her first step imprinted on my heart,
Her footprints etch gopadma* on my heart
Her laughter like the ringing of temple bells
She spills joy, and I am mystified
Is this the doll I made? Ragged, sundry, common!
I made her to vindicate, validate myself, stubbornly
How did she turn out so talented, so charming?
How did I grow to love her so, as she loves me?
It's a wonder, this change in my life
Disrupting my game
I must set the board afresh for her
New game, new pawns, the play my responsibility
She is my work, my leisure
She is my strength, my energy.

---

* A cow's hoof print drawn as a rangoli motif, a holy symbol.

Five

She has grown, filled out now
Chubby and adorable, skipping around
In the neighbourhood, some have been kind, others critical
Some have pointed 'This is *that* doll!'
'Oh, I see!' 'I thought as much,
She does seem different.' She from others
She does not understand what they are saying
But senses the discrimination
Through the pity, scorn, the sideways looks,
Words with unmistakable inference
Confused, frightened, she retreats
Into the cocoon of my embrace
Where she finds safety, sanctuary
A protective armour like that of Karna's
Where did he get it? Legend says from his father
Or from mother Kunti, but I know
For certain, he got it from Radha
Who fostered him in her love
Loving him beyond life
Turning him into Radheya, her son.
I did the same with my doll
Gathering her in my arms, safe from the world

I cut a piece from my cape of tolerance and patience
And designed a dress for my doll
How beautiful she looked! I snap my fingers to ward off evil
Provoking mocking laughter, 'Evil smiting evil?'
But they don't know, my ears are wind tunnels
Blowing out the litter of rough words
Why won't she be smitten?
Don't the stars and the moon
Envy her? Salt, mustard, scorn, hatred, pity
I grasp firmly in my hands and circle them over her
To fling them far way, she has to be tough
Swimming upstream with me, she'll need all her luck.

It's time to take her into the herd on the board
To acquire features like them, eyes, ears, hands and legs
Perhaps a tail, maybe she will need one to wag at times!
She will have to learn the rules of the game, their ways
Straight columns forward and backward and crossways
They may not welcome her, but I will have to push her
In her new dress, I begin to lead her

Once again the dissection of our relationship
Again the ignominy, the insult, the humiliation
Satisfied, they say, 'You may go now
We shall take care of her, teach her how…'

Her fist tight around my forefinger
I unwrap with all the determination I can muster
I glance back, despite myself, her lost look
Brimming eyes, hands reaching out to me
My heart a stone, resolutely I walk away
Closing the door behind me, releasing her into the fray

Six

She found playmates, my doll, and happiness
In the herd, with others, themselves dolls
With names and addresses and legitimacy
Beautiful, proper dolls, innocent for lack of experience
She played, sang and danced with them
With starry anklets tinkling
Seeming a part of them, there was no difference
Dolling her up everyday, I would lead her to the herd
Innocent and eager, she would readily join them

She had no name, no address
These I gave, my playmate consented
Why should she be nameless now?
Why should she be gameless?

I relaxed and rested my careworn head
On my partner's shoulders, he too is a part of the game!
My doll is his too, but she is yet small,
Now the path from home to herd is well beaten
Hardened by step after step, a linking thread
Travelled by my calloused feet and her tiny tread

I wondered everyday, seeing her off at the herd
Is this the same feeble, sickly doll?
Plump and healthy now, dressed smartly
Carrying her satchel and water bottle expertly
Not to forget the lunch lovingly packed
I was happy that I had made her happy
Now she will move with the group
I have choreographed her dance with the troupe
Safe in this knowledge, I walk the path from home to herd
With blinkers on my eyes, doubts unheard
Quite suddenly, one day I stopped and turned
My heart missed a beat, the yard so lonely
Not a soul in sight, I panicked for her
I pushed open the gate, went up to the door
Running in out of turn, an unexpected move

The door creaks open as if unwilling
My eyes racing ahead looking for her
'Are you all right, my darling?
Why don't I hear your notes in the chorus?
Where is the tint of your lips in this rainbow of words?
Why can't I see your glossy head in this sea of dark ones?
Where are you? Has the earth swallowed you?
Or have the walls and the ceiling vaulted you?
Where are you? Where are you?'
Agonised, I enter the herd, my eyes still searching
I find her with her face to the wall, feeling
The heartless stone with hesitant fingers
Satchel, bottle, paraphernalia undisturbed
My tears well up, 'Why so?' I ask

'Why hasn't she been unsaddled, let loose to play
Run free, why isn't she singing? Laughing? Dancing?'
'She is strange, eccentric, weird,
She doesn't want to learn, she doesn't respect rules
She wants to be unfettered, grow wild like a weed.'
'Dearest!' cried my heart and she turned
Collecting her in my arms, I held her tightly
Searching her face for the reason
I saw it clearly mirrored in her sequestered eyes
My name growing faint on her lost expression
I held her even tighter, trying to imprint it again
I asked them to leave, for her sake
The door of the herd slightly ajar,
They did heed this, but perhaps only because
They wanted her to slip out, never to return!

Resolutely disengaging her arms tight around me
Holding her baby face up to me,
I whispered the mantra in her reluctant ears
'Whether you are lonely or with friends,
You will have to learn the rules of the game
For my sake, please, as much as you can, even with your face
Turned away.... Will you please, my darling?'
My good little doll agreed, nodding her understanding
I retraced my heavy steps with a heavier heart
Leaving her behind, stepping into my footprints
She followed me, through the door, through the gate
I had no courage to stop her
I had no heart to send her back.

Now she would hear the echoing sound of me calling
Her name, she would wait to catch the faint rustle
Of my step, with lightning speed she would leave the herd
And run to me, a prodigal homecoming everyday.
I decided to preserve this primal pull
She was dearer to me than any rule
Of the game, of fate, she was dear only to me
I had done my duty of introducing her to the herd
Now it was up to her, learning, singing, playing
Even conforming.

Seven

I was still charmed.
As fascinated by the doll as she was by me
Wasn't I fulfilling my other duties, working, resting
Socialising, as and when I could break the spell?
Spending time with my playmate late at night
When dreams settled gently on my doll's eyelids.
I was deaf to complaints, blind to distance
So smitten was I, my world enchanted by my doll
Her mere touch strummed the strings of my heart
My eyes recorded only her beautiful image
My hands engaged in pursuits around her
The running stitches tacking her existence to mine
Appearing as intricate as patterns on her dress
With the needle provided by my mate
I embroidered motifs coloured by my bleeding fingers.
I dressed her in varied apparel, silk, satin, wool, cotton
Changing as often as our moods

I marvel at her sandalwood perfection
Holding her close to my heart, kissing her
My body soaks in the aroma of incense
In making her, I transgressed onto a crooked path

Flanked by the alluring lush plants of the Kewra[*].
I am caught in the clouds of her curls
By rainbow ribbons of affection
She smiles sunnily at me with ruby lips
And a sweet sharp pain rips through my heart
'Let my game end now!'

This moment is a gold coin
To be treasured, safely knotted in my torn pallav[†]
I am so happy I could die now,
Before the moment spills, before the coin slips....

I thrill at her touch, and suddenly realise
She has left her childhood behind
Her touch is no longer baby-soft, childlike
She is flowering, her flesh taut with her youth
Curves like tightly wrapped buds
Her expression has a softness, her chin a sharp outline
A new grace to her step, as if to conquer the world
As in the first sunlight a dew-soaked bud
Unfurling a petal from its tight embrace,
So will a new horizon appear with the sunrise
Promising a new world, and the bud mesmerised
Such is the state of my beloved princess

---

* Pandanus (screwpine) which has a heady scent.

† loose end of a sari, women often tie keys or coins into the pallav for
safekeeping.

She blushes rose red
Her toys now a thing of the past.

I watch her keenly like the sleepless, watching for the
Blooming of the elusive Bramha Kamal[*]
And delicately preserve that moment
Of her blossoming, engraved in my heart
Wiping the tears on her velvet cheeks
With my roughened hands, my words as drops
Gentle in her sculpted ears
'Dearest doll, you shall wear my bangle
And cover yourself with my pallav
I shall watch your step, your blossoming,
You will not be just mine now
My doll, my daughter, my life
You will have your own play board now
Something to mark your completeness
You are now a woman, adimata[†]
It's all part of His game.'
As I say this, a sharp pain sears my heart
Amidst all this celebration, where,
Where is my little doll? My baby?

---

[*] the mythical elusive flower of Bramha, the creator of the universe, which blooms once in fourteen years, at night and for a very short period

[†] primal mother

Eight

She's as tall as I am, perhaps taller
Treading the same beaten path with
Shoes now my size, to reach the herd
But I am at home seeing her off
And greeting her when she returns
She is still the same, playful, at times,
Clumsy, butterfingered, falling into
My arms and narrating the day's events
Mother this and Mother that, poking fun
Worrying, competing, enjoying,
I wait for all this, hand in hand with the sun
Moving from the east to the west
Fretting about her, relaxing when she returns
My dusk illuminated till long after
She can hardly bear this separation
She and I, the two of us, bathing, basking
In the gentle light of dawn and dusk
Snuggling under the dark sequined shawl
Oblivious to the world
Awakened only by the first rays
I was spinning carefree in this happiness
Unprepared, unsuspecting, a little selfish, too!
Her presence delicately
Untangling the complex bonds, at a distance
I observe her closely, a shiver, a wave

Spasms through my being, why is she
So indifferent, cold, withdrawn, unfamiliar?
Looking at me with alien eyes
Her expression so strange, all references
Of relationships fast vanishing from her touch
I can see her recede, like a mirage
'My doll! Why this? I am Mother, your mother.
Where are you disappearing into this vast unknown?
You'll get lost with no hope of return!
Look! Look into my eyes, into my heart
You'll see myriad images of yourself
Installed as if in the sanctum sanctorum.
Look at the flow of my blood
Can you see the currents of my love
Coursing through my body?
These hands that cradled you, the lullaby
I hummed still rests on my lips
Do you remember the cool breeze
Fanned by my eyelashes on hot, clammy days
On your feverish skin?
Do you remember the welcoming warmth of my lap
And more importantly, the heat of ambition, the zest for life
That seeped into you from my embrace?'

'When you walked through the thorny thickets of my life
I spread out my palms under your beautiful feet
Lest they bled, shall I prove my love
With the wounds on the back of my hands?'

Her look speared through my heart
The first glimmer of condescension
In her hitherto believing eyes
Scoffing at my pitiable attempts to account
Trying to dispel the expression in a hurry
I appealed, 'Say, Mother, my Mother!'
Our usual game drew no response
No affection, no intimacy, no sign
Of her being mine
Icy eyes looking away
A mechanical, 'Mother, my Mother'
An edict ending our relationship
She disappears into the distance
And I, fully conscious of my loss
Astounded, looking back
My bundle of joy and sorrow I had
Carefully brought along so far
Fallen away somewhere along the path
Enthralled by my doll I walked ahead
All alone on this desolate path
Forsaking everything, leaving it all behind
And she trying to escape from me
Desperate, I try to pick up
The pearls rolling all over the sand
A futile task, a defeated me.

Nine

I cannot rest now, I have to examine
Everything from the beginning
What went wrong, where I slipped up
My knit and purl. I knew my limits
Did I not plan accordingly? In making her
I had selected the best, cleanest rags
Chaste, pure, tested by my love
Untainted threads had stitched her together
Even after she was made, I had never
Kept her away, but merged her
Into me, consciously, deliberately
I tried to give her whatever I had
Veracity, purity, virtue, I tried to
Inculcate in her, striving to protect her
From my faults and foibles
I led her hand to form the shree[*]
I still treasure that holy memory
Deep within my heart.

I had never reserved any emotion
Whilst making her mine, never was able to…
I toiled with my blood and sweat

---

* A letter symbolising an auspicious beginning.

And this strange expression in her eyes today
As if I were nobody.
Granted she said 'I am yours'
Agreed, she called me Mother
But her tone, so distant, so dry
And why did she not look me in the eye?
Why didn't I see the earlier celebration
That lit up her face with my name?
Why didn't her eyes sparkle with moonbeams
When she said she was mine?
Why did her words ring so hollow?
Why did she break away from me?
Why this distance, which seeks to destroy our world?

I reached out, stroking her beloved head
Which I had so tenderly groomed
Kissed her lovingly and asked her
Hesitantly, as if skinning my heart
'My doll, why are you cross with me?
What do you want? Tell me, and you
Shall have it! Just tell me.'
'I want my mother!' replied she
Flicking off my clinging affection
Discarding, rejecting my love.
I was numb, confused, perplexed
I reached out to touch her
Drawing my anguish from the depths of my heart
I appealed to her, tremulous,
'What do you mean, my dearest?
Isn't this a strange quest?

I am right here, very much here, your Mother!'
My longing evident, my tone helpless
And my sincerity
Struggling to find that chink in her armour.
She relented a little, confronting me
Reached out to pat my head, and said
'No, that's not what I mean. You have deluded
Yourself and me, all along. I am not yours.
Did He give me to you? Where did you get me?
Tell me! Who are my parents? My progenitors?
Why did you keep this from me?'
I went berserk, distressed and despairing
My ego shattered
I had made her, with all my precious rags
Crafted her carefully, thought her mine
As I was hers, I swear on my life
I am her mother! Her mother!
My playmate had to accept her
Along with me, a condition of our game
Where can I get her another mother?
How can I calm her? How can I placate her?
Salvaging the vestiges of my strength
I stood there, as before
Empty-handed

I collect the dregs of my pride
Together with the empty, kernel-less shells
Of words, and lay them shamefacedly
In front of her and plead,
'My dearest, I have no answers for your

Soul-racking queries, I stand here
In front of you, the desire to be called "Mother"
By you, deep-seated, deep-rooted in me.
Now it's for you to decide
But I give you this critical caution
Don't disregard, for reasons however compelling
My heart that I have laid bare for you
Do you not see your reflection there?
My existence is meaningless without you
Not just for me, but for my mate too
Dearest decide, whether we are to live or die!'
My wise little doll.
She deliberated, decided, and with wisdom beyond her years
Comforted me, 'Have I not called you "Mother"
From the time I gained awareness?
And have I ever distanced the playmate?
And am I going to leave you?
How can I and where will I go?
Come; let me wipe your tears,
We shall be together, for all our years.'

She said this, and moved away
Quietly, with stooping shoulders, disappearing
Consoling me with a pittance of words
Robbed of the affection of ages
How didn't I realize she was like a fruit
Plucked raw from the tree, bleeding
Her wound deeper than mine, leaching
A lifetime of taunts and digs, suddenly making
Sense, references to illegitimacy

Getting contexts clear
She needs me now, my care
Soothing zephyrs of my breath to salve
Her primal wounds
But I realised it was futile, useless
Intense desolation orphaned her
Almost snapping her ties rooted here
Wounded, mangled, she moved around
Directionless, suspended
I comfort her with my inadequate hands
And she reciprocates, ineffectively
How can I convince her of my love?
How can I tell her to abandon
The futile attempt to extricate herself
Like separating grains of sugar
From the milk
'Agreed you were denied my milk
But did my nourishing love not seep through
When I held you to my heart tight?
Then why this suspicion, this dreadful doubt?
I have not given birth to you
But my life I have devoted to you
Then why does this emptiness fill you?
How can I tell you, we are entwined inextricably?
Braided tightly, endlessly?'
I yearned that she could sense this without words
But she was beyond words, impregnable

I grant you this, my doll, sulk, brood, remain distanced
Moving around like a stranger

Trying to disengage yourself from my bonds
Do as you please, show me your edges
Corners and sides, keep to yourself
And I to myself, keeping a watchful eye
On my injured calf, guarding with my life
Unmindful of doubts and questions
Sleepless you toss around, even as the moon rises
I shall embalm your lacerations with sandal* paste
And sing your favourite lullaby
As long as you harbour the grudge,
I, your mother, shall stand silent sentinel.

---

* An aromatic wood, considered sacred and medicinal.

Ten

I soothe my frayed mind with the lullaby
that I sang for her, once sung for me
by my mother and hers for her.
As I sing, a sense of calm washes over me
Cleansing every fibre of my being
Through my clearing thoughts I see
The truth, clear, unclouded
Her blood and mine of one colour
But her life had begun in a strange womb,
Abandoned disinterestedly to the unknown.
I will never be able to hold her
With my tireless and hopeful ties
Her blood, which I nurtured, not really mine
I can only transfuse, irrigate, revitalise
I can show her as evidence
My bleeding at her incised wounds
She will not deny the debt
Of my troubles and tribulations for her
She will concede this, she will love me
She will do all that is necessary
She will cherish the name I gave her
I know, she is beyond ingratitude

Yes, she will do this, but that's not enough for me
I have not striven only for this
I want her to be involved in me,
Exist mainly for me, but this is slowly changing
She entered my life like a bright ray of sunrise
Now she is vanishing gradually like the
Lengthening shadows of sunset
Bringing another day to a close.

In the house where she toddled on her little feet
Leaving imprints on my heart and hands
She now moves around like a refugee
Housed in a shelter, a temporary guest
No demands for indulgence
She doesn't relish anything I get for her
As if she has no needs, no wants
I cook with love and care
Favourite dishes and fare
Packing them for when she goes out to the herd
She brings them back, untouched as she is by hunger
No longer drawn to home
On hot afternoons, missing her, full of wanting
I am pulled to the herd
In search of her, puffing and panting
To see her by the barbed fence
Staring into the dark clouded sky

'Darling, why do you stand like this lost?'
I draw her to me
She swiftly looks at me, the knives of her cold stares
Slicing through my false bravado.
Shards of pain shoot through her heart too
She helps me collect my tattered courage
'Look, how the storm clouds gather
I was watching them, scared of the darkness
I wish a wind would blow away these clouds
Or that rain would fall, washing everything down.'
'Yes, my dear, so it should, this darkness
This uneasiness, these stuffed clouds
All should go away, leaving behind
The warm rays of the morning sun.'

I speak, she speaks, she asks, I ask
Sometimes her answer, sometimes mine
Mere rituals, both of us observe the customs
The decorum, a lifetime of habits, routine
But she doesn't blossom as before
Doesn't hug me anymore
Whispering, pouting, giggling, teasing
Gluttony, mischief, disobedience she has suspended
Hung as if on a peg, and she waiting
For that moment of escape,
That chance of distancing.
I was filled with pity, my poor darling
Her age of joyfulness and play
Cut short so cruelly
By this lonely burden of searching

For her existence, her origins, her being
A quest slowly, inexorably destroying.

She doesn't remember the words I taught her
The rhymes and songs I sang with her
Sulk in her solemn cheeks
She avoids my playmate, her game indecipherable
As if playing hide and seek with him
Like she plays blind man's buff with me.
She goes to the herd, but then crosses
The barbed fence into the world beyond.
There I am told, she doesn't stay in the herd
Doesn't learn the rules of the game of the board
Defeated, I question her, she doesn't listen
Words our weapons, skirmishes innumerable
With my playmate she remains distanced
My friends advise, 'Stop pampering her
Discipline her, rein her in and see
How she comes on track.' Yet others
Remind me, 'See, Did we not warn you?
Such dolls are wretches, ingrates,
Did we not caution you?
They should be kept subdued, suppressed
Controlled and punished
Did we not advise you?'

'You allowed yourself to be carried away
And left a pile of questions unanswered

Problems for your mate to solve.
Why?
All is not lost, rein her in, pull hard at the bit
And don't loosen your grip till you tether
Her to some suitable, strong lad.'
Some said with biting sarcasm, 'You made her
Out of rebellion, with old rags, the poor mite
But you regret it now, your affection ebbing
She is silly, unable to learn
The rules of the game of life and yet you
Are unaffected, thriving, enjoying
Mingling with your herd in their revelry
As if nothing was the matter, pretending.
Oh, yes, you must have got a chattel
An unpaid servant to do your bidding.'
But some commiserated, 'This too shall pass
Wipe your tears and tighten your belt
The dross will settle down, the whirlwind
Will pass, and she will be yours once again.'

Eleven

I decided to wait for the storm to pass
And the lull to come
Tongues wagged, criticism abounded
I relied on Him, for a solution
I had wronged Him, let Him now mete out
The punishment for my transgression.
Whether she realizes this or not
I know, the mere thought of her makes
My heart unfold, petal by petal
The rhymes I composed for her echo
Through the corridors of my being
Ignorant, uneducable, unskilled she may be
Wild, uncontrollable, uncultured
Or old in years and deeds
For me she is still my innocent little baby
A tiny butterfly settled on my palm
I have no strength to put her to test
Nor do I have the heart to beat
Or berate her into submission
I yearn for her to consider herself mine.
Yet I don't have the courage to impose belonging
My playmate and He know only too well
How she is so much a part of my being
But I do not know how to seek
Evidence of my belonging in her being.

I had never stopped her steps
Never used the leash of love to hold her in check
I never wanted her to fall out of step with me
But I would never have stopped her had she done so
I didn't want her to be trapped in me
Like a bee in the petal prison of the lotus
I always wanted her to be free
Like the butterfly, floating at will
I wanted her to be happy thus
I wanted to spread my work-roughened hands
On the barbed-wire fence, lest she tear
Her soft wings, I would bear the pain
Or not feel at all, my senses numbed
Alive only to her existence

Despite this
She entered the forbidden woods
Tempted by gaudy yellow flowers
Overcome by their wild fragrance
Intoxicated by their heady scent
Entrapped by sharp nettles renting
Lasciviously through her flesh.
I lit the lamps of my eyes in search
Of her in the maze
And found him, crude, brute
Casting a spell of black magic
On my innocent darling, so lovingly fostered

He planned to savage her, devour her
I stumbled like a sleepwalker
Rudely awakened
And she had gone so far away
How did I miss her inflorescence?
Ah, but she had let it bloom secretly
In the deep crevices of her heart
She had experienced the effect of her wile
Of artful charming, she had practised
Her weapons once before, the success heady!
Now she was playing a game so fiery.

My hurt soul cried out from the depths
Writhing with the stinging pain
'My dearest, we shall untangle the mystery
Whether you are mine and I am yours
Later, but I have not raised you
so you can give in so easily
And waste yourself in futile pursuits
You have to peak to newer heights
Take courage from the bright sun in the east
Look, when the time is right
I will guide you to your destination
Lead you to safety;
Do you think I do not want to see your game set?
Be careful amidst the thorns
Let me take you to a bower happy
There build a nest
Lined with feathers, and find you a playmate
Handsome and worthy.

Don't be misled by the piper
Not your match, a mere traveller
He will charm you away, play you till the edge
You are a flower lovingly nurtured
How can I bear to see you tortured?'

I talked, breathless, drenched in sweat
Then lost, defeated, I tried to stop her
But she stood her ground, staring at me
Fearless and daring
Her dry loveless tone left me speechless
'Why do you pretend to care?
Don't you want to be rid of me?
Why is he bad, unsuitable?
Because he has no name? Do I have one?
You lent me yours
But I don't want this dead skin
Nameless as we are, we will write one name together
And survive somehow in the game
We shall not be indebted to anyone
Hungry we shall be, but our hearts will be filled
With our love, his love for me
Will lack the lustre of the love you showered
But will not have a list of travails suffered
There shall be streams of pure feelings
Springing only for me.
No, you don't have the power to stop me
I walked with you because I was lonely
Now at these crossroads, I have company

Let me go now! Leave me to my fate
Bid me farewell, this is my destiny.'

She spoke thus, and I stood transfixed
A bolt of lightning coursed through me
With the realization, the humiliation
This chit of a doll reigned over my world
I chose her over others, those close to me
I had fed her with my love, staked everything for her
Never counting, despite what she says.
Let her slander, but I am her mother
Whether or not she acknowledges it, she is mine
My responsibility, I have to act now and suck
The venom from her before it turns her blue
Before it destroys our world, throws our nest askew
Reason was defeated, now I grew wild
Thrashing her, lashing at her, taming her
I bled! I flagellated myself
'What have you brought us to?
The game I had begun with firm resolve
To win, against all odds
You are forcing the result, the defeat
Where did I go wrong?
Did my lullaby slip a note?'

Drained of strength and spirit we both
Lick our wounds, on our bodies and in our hearts
'Don't you dare cross my threshold

Nor jump the fence of the herd
Don't you dare step out of the circle.'

She turns, to my relief, obediently
I am weeping, she drying her tears resolutely
I cry silently to her, 'My dearest doll
You are running after a mirage
Into the unknown, in search of the unseen
Can't you see the springs of my love,
Don't they gurgle to you?
Are you inured? Immune?'

Twelve

The house is now a prison
Dark, claustrophobic, she, I
And my partner flitting around
Silent, ghostly figures, distracted
Searching for shards of past happiness
Scraps of contentment in empty corners
She has lost every memory, every reference
Of the past, the present, and the future
Disoriented, lost, aimless
We watch helplessly, my playmate
Even more confused, incapacitated
Hurting from within, with limitless love
For me, for our doll
We live and move in darkness
Doors and windows shut tight
Yet some noises escape through the chinks
'It seems they beat her heartlessly
Would they if she were their own?'

'But she deserved it, the wretch!
She was fostered in care
But she showed her true colours
The inferior blood proving itself!'

'We had warned her, you see
Look, this is slush, scum, filth
You won't be able to deal with it
Trying to drape it in riches
Will only bring you misery.'

'She put up the pretence of being a mother
Little did she know it wouldn't be easy
She should have known the fragility
After all, blood lasts, not water.'

The chinks deepened, the voices seeped in
Till they overcame us, a cacophony of
Opinions, advice, comments unsolicited
Killing my motherhood,
Taunting my partner's paternity
And deriding her for being a daughter.
We three lost souls lorn
Mazing our way through thistle and thorn
Where there were no paths
Only cold ends, like death itself.

More assuaging than the living
Cradling us on waves of peace
Painless, peaceful, eternal sleep.
The ultimate truth, the certainty and reality
Of life, leaving behind the travails

The obligations, the scars
I didn't give birth to my doll
But she can die with me.
And my playmate, silent, enduring
Our pain, valiantly trying to shield us
How could we embark on this ultimate journey
Into the vast unknown, without him?

I rose, calmly filled three chalices
With sweet, dark, hemlock
We sat in front of each other
And I asked 'My dearest, you will drink this, won't you?'
She nodded her affirmation and lowered her lids
Brimming with tears
And we raised our goblets in a toast
To our deadly journey into the unknown
I looked at her, determined, intrepid.
Her courage, her resolve when facing the ultimate
Flashed a spark in me
It was not in vain, what I strove to give her
She has the strength to bear mountains
Of sorrow, the seeds I sowed in her
Germinating, did I have the right now
To wither them before time?
I set her on the board in my need, my greed
But the moves are played by Him
Should I cheat her out of her turn?
My hearts desire to see her in her prime
Why should I take her before her time?

I threw away the death drink
Framed the luminous orb of her face with my palms
I looked at her limpid eyes, poured assurance
Into her, 'No my dearest doll, we can't give up now
We shall fight this out, together
My hands and your two
The body is not chaff, to be allowed to blow
Away in the whirlwind.'
She hungrily returned my gaze
Questions arising there
'Am I like you? Yours? In your image?'
'Yes, my dearest, you are like me,
Mine, in my image, and I am all yours
Along with my playmate!'

A stranger journey was never embarked upon
By a pair like us, with the mate
Teasing the throes of death
We had explored with our world-weary eyes
The shores of that great ocean serene
Glass-topped, fathomless and fearsome
It would have devoured us without a ripple.

Exhaustion overcame us
As if we had walked miles
In this arduous journey
Body and soul awash with fatigue
Inside and outside all swelling into one

Eager to reveal layer by layer
Whatever remained in the recesses of our hearts
We seized this poignant moment
Casting our selves aside
Soothing the bleeding wounds
With salubrious love
And the cooling breath of care
Appeasing, stroking our battered egos.
I had thought I knew all there was to her
Watching her grow day by day
An intrinsic part of me
Was I not naïve and presumptuous?
But as she uncorked hidden phials
Of pent up emotions
And poured out the heaps of her love
For me, I realized our existence
Was meaningless without each other

A deadly green snake hissed
Distrust out of the depths of her heart
I made her out of rags, made her mine
But did I anchor her with unswerving security
That I would not desert her at the bend?
That I would not erase the name I had given her?
Doubts she harboured since her individuation
Ominous shadows hovering over her
As she drifted unwanted, insecure

I stumbled at her pain
And vowed, 'My dearest, I know
Where I lacked, fell short
I couldn't give you the warmth of trust
That seeps through a mother's milk
Into her beloved young one
But it is there, my dearest
Filled within me, for you, reserved for you
You'll feel the love, I am certain, before my end
And germinate a seedling in you,
Filling you with transparent pure love
And then, testing my love on that touchstone
You will realise, my love for you was
Not inferior, no less, in any way
I made you with rags from deep within
Only to bequeath them to you, to love
And cherish you more than I would ever myself.
I am not upset, 'tis but a rule of the game
To throw, sow seeds of doubt
I give you no responsibility or blame
That these seeds of grass took root
In the impressionable credulous soil of your mind
Growing unhindered within you, choking you
My fault that I did not weed them out
I shall do that now, very tenderly
Carefully removing these insidious roots
Without bruising you,
It will happen, certainly one day!
Until then I will not impose, or expect
Even until dark I will wait
For I know the water lily opens
At night, petal by bright petal

Its gentle fragrance wafting out
I want to ensure each petal blooms
No canker curling its corners
I will search for screens and separators
That keep us from each other, and
Will them to crumble
Dusting away the cobwebs, I must be careful
Not to wipe away the signs of your new
Awareness of self, yet preserving unbroken
That one tenacious silk thread that binds
You to me forever
I wish the link of being that ends with me
Is forged by you, to the chain
Of existence till the end of this world
My flesh is mortal, but I want you to carry
My life wish, my sensibility, my ambition
Flowing through you to your progeny
And then will you understand, someday
You had a mother who filled you with these
Who didn't give birth to you
But lived in every pore of your body.

Thirteen

The long dark night relents
And makes space for dawn
My dawn too came with the sun
Sickly pale yellow at first, as if after the eclipse
Then with bright, aureate rays
I rose with alacrity, shedding skin
There is much to do
I have responsibilities and tasks
My doll's future is at stake

Then I get busy, swing into action
To fulfil vows I had made
Our goal now to settle our dearest
On a certain path she has to tread
My partner and I work night and day
We have reached thus far, brought her along
To this stage, struggling, erring, faltering
But it is the rule of the game that a fruit
Ripe and ready, should not remain
On the tree, there is no in point that
This treasured fruit we had so lovingly nurtured
Should fall down and spoil and bruise

Or be partaken on the tree by marauding birds

I opened all the doors and windows
To let the light stream in
My mind and heart as clear as crystal
Why do I hide from the light?
Whatever the matter, it is transparent
Nothing shameful, no truth unpleasant
But it was not easy I knew
To search for a destination for my beloved
To explore the boundaries of the possible
I wanted to place her gently there
To ripen as would the seeds inside her
I wanted her to shine and glow
Fulfilled, contented, as did everyone else.

Even if it grows dark, I have vowed
To fill my eyes with light
And in the dim glow, seek out for her
An abode as solid and safe as mine
There must be one, earmarked
For my beloved somewhere on this earth,
Where someone is waiting for her
Just as eager and desperate.
He who denied me a doll
Surely will not be so heartless
As to deny a playmate to my doll?

Perhaps, it is possible, that this is a move
On the scoreboard of life, perhaps I am destined
To do what He means me to!
I shall do this, I will for sure
And find the right match for her
Someone to give her the love and care she so richly deserves

And so I got down to work
As did my playmate with me
Misled for a moment, we followed
The beaten track of the horoscope
And background, profile and photograph
Yet again the butt of mockery and joke
How do I search for the star signs
Of my darling, herself as beautiful as a star?
We have only vague references of her past
How can we build her future on them?
I believe my lineage is hers
I wish that others would too, including
My family, but I have no right
To insist.
But is this the right path? Not for us is
The narrow beaten track
Instead I must look around in the wilderness
To spy a thorny shrub as desolate
As myself, willing to approve of
Me and my mate along with my doll
A mate of her own
It will be difficult, but not impossible

My patience and endurance on trial
I trudged steadfast, unmindful of the sharp spikes stabbing me
The double-edged ridicule of my doll and I
'This strange pair, mother and daughter
Searching for someone like them
To carry on the line of immorality
A home as forsaken as theirs!'
The insidious intent of these words
Seeping in like poisonous fumes
We filtered out with masks of patience
Perseverance, faith, I continued my quest
The search for a home for my doll
A solid home, filled with real people
Bristly from the outside while
Hiding springs of unlimited love
For my doll, I found one
As elusive as the mythical jewel on the
King Cobra's luminous hood,
So alive and thriving, that I ran to it
Shrugging off all my lethargy
Garnering all the humility
I ever possessed, I asked for it,
That shining, precious, elusive jewel
For my doll, dearer than life.
For someone who had to struggle
For virtually everything in life, it was surprisingly
Easy to find him, like lopping off a ripe fruit.
My tears welled up to celebrate
The moment with me, caressing
My doll's cheek I asked her
'My dearest, do you like your
New playmate that I have selected?'

I read her acquiescence on her lowered lids
Through the sheer curtain of her tears
Misty, yet a crystal clear 'yes'
So trusting, resting so credulously
On my reassuring, dependable love.

Fourteen

Standing at the golden threshold
Of that chosen house I scoured
Every nook and corner
I smelled the fragrance of the breeze
Wafting over the prajakta[*] flowers in the yard
Mixing gently with the heady scent of the bakul[†]
The beams of the rising and setting sun
Lighting, illuminating every sconce
I spied a swing moving gently
On a cool neem[‡] tree.
A mother figure for my doll here
A father too, like my mate
And a playmate of her own
To bathe in the fragrance, play on the swing
To bask in the sunshine, to whisper sweet nothings
My dearest will set up her home here
Will spent her days gloriously
The nights magical, counting
Moonbeams with her soulmate.

---

* Night-flowering jasmine, considered sacred

† Indian Medlar, a fragrant flower that is considered sacred

‡ Indian Lilac, a medicinal tree

My dearest has served her banishment
A new era of happiness will now begin
Pain, hurt, wounds, tears: things of past!
My heart was filled, I stepped into that home
And to those who gathered around me
I laid open to them, my love for my doll,
And pleaded with them to grant her a place
Isn't the fourth corner still empty?
She will occupy only that but,
Will fill your hearts with affection.
While calling her your own
Why do we need to make deals of dowry?
My wealth of a lifetime and that of my mate
Gathered bit by bit over the hard years
Only to be spent on our dearest!
What is ours is hers to spend
A provision for the unknown future
Does one greet with a heavy heart
The bright rise of the new day?
My slowly darkening horizon
Shall never limit her bright ascent in the sky
Once she is in the fourth corner
Wrapping, touching you all with her love
And I might, if anything, only assist
I promise, my existence shall never intrude
From my corner of her heart, yet I know
She will always treasure that corner
While she embarks on her new life

※

As if sensing my silent manifest
That house nodded its assent
I searched through the depths of my mind
And came up with the most propitious time
For the wedding of my beloved daughter
A huge marquee, limitless as my love,
As the sky, we put up in the yard
Propped by green plantain pillars
Loaded with the plump, ripe fruit of good wishes
I gathered all that I had, rich clothes
Perfumes, jewellery, flowers and adorned her
And yes, I remembered the glazed green glass bangles
For the auspicious start of her new life.
Marking her luminous forehead with the tilak
As radiant as the sun, I beseeched Him
'She has embarked on the board
With seven significant steps, hand in hand
With her own mate. You know I am ready
To relinquish in your favour all the punya*,
The merit, I have accrued over the years
Please take care that her path
Is not waylaid by prickly thorns
I have packed for her journey
Aspirations colourful, just like mine
Take care she doesn't stumble
And spill those in the sand
You have caused her suffering
Tormented her limitlessly, please put an end
To those game penalties, of running

---

* A Hindu concept of good deeds or merit

Cross-country across mountains and vales
Let her now flow peacefully, happily.'

I invited the whole town
To the wedding celebrations
Of my beloved daughter
And they came, at the holy hour
To witness the fruition, the culmination
Of my timeless one-legged penance
Some came with clean hearts
Others out of sense of obligation
To throw a few grains of confetti
Still others came to watch the fun
Ridiculing, disparaging, 'Who's the mother,
Who's the father and who's the daughter?
A strange threesome, enacting the farce
Of a lifetime, this is the climax of their act!'
With pressed lips, concealing their sneers
They too joined the festivities
But I wasn't worried
I wanted to prove to everyone
My doll, who had been declared
Dumb, immature, strange, inconsequential
But extremely important and dear to me
Had been given a playmate by Him
Someone as beautiful and charming as her
I knew as I propped the slender vine
On to the lattice to grow freely
The lips and hearts of those who care for me
Uttered their blessings, their hands bade farewell
I knew it was the wealth of a lifetime

Ever replenishing, ever renewing
Like the old woman's little pot of faith
And piety showered endlessly on the Shiva Linga[*]
Amidst the corrupt offerings of others.

As I watched my dearest place
The garland around her mate's neck
Something snapped deep inside me
The hands and the lips of my near ones
Consoling and supporting
I bore with unknown, untapped strength
That testing moment of our parting
Of my uprooting, with help from this
Very wealth of my lifetime
Determinedly unwrapping her tight embrace
Wiping her tears, while letting mine flow freely
Turning her away and catching that handful of
Rice, symbolising the breaking of ties
My mate and I stood there with our hearts
In our eyes, and said, 'Farewell darling doll,
Go home to your people, where you belong now
Cross that golden threshold rightfully
The mistress of that household
Reigning supreme there, in the house
To which you now belong
Go on ahead, progress
Don't fear anything, dearest
Move forward with your own people

---

[*] A representation of the Hindu deity Shiva

They will lead you to the distant horizon
And I shall watch over you
Like a mother hawk, soaring high,
Keeps on her chick a vigilant eye.'

Fifteen

She's gone, my doll has gone
To her house, her very own
Her affection and anger, learning and not learning
Crying and laughing, hugging and sulking
All these, or her very being there
Had filled my house, my heart, my whole self
She dragged it away along with her
Like a queen trailing her train behind her
Taking in its sway the peace of my house
I ran from this door to the other,
Window to window, searching for the remnants,
The signs of her being, finding an ornament
Here and a garment there, a dried tuberose
Worn and discarded by her, even
The old broken slippers she had thrown away.
I gathered nostalgically from her things,
Memories spilling like the scent of the bakul
Holding them to my heart I stood
Under the champa, my eyes closed,
And heard prancing footsteps!
I thought I would feel the embrace
Of her dainty arms, feel her scented breath
On my ears, hurriedly whispering some secret
I thought she would hold my hands
And make some demands sweet

Or sit at the table, hungry and tired
And ask to be fed her favourite cream and sugar
Mind-reader as she is, she knows
That's what I really want too
She's gone away, gone away far
This is true, very true, and yet

She is here, with me, in me
This is also true, equally true
I don't need any company, any presence
In the house keeps me from
Stitching together her memories, it clouds my thoughts
Of her, they called me eccentric
Shunning everyone, keeping to myself
But I paid no heed, I had no time
I had to pick, before the end of day
The flowers falling to the ground
Social obligations, a mere waste of time
I had enjoyed her being here tremendously
Now I had to enjoy intensely
Her not being here, too, her presence
And absence had to be respected
Equally, seriously, regally.

While relishing the sweet agony
Of her absence, slowly, excruciatingly
A geyser of desire shot through me
To see that vine resting peacefully, thriving

To extinguish that spark of longing
By meeting her, the content happy image of her

I hurried to her happy, prosperous home
Searching for signs of her past in her, while she
Fussed over me amidst the welcoming others
Scouring secret signs of familiarity
Scanning her less unsure movements
Raking her mirror-transparent expression
And yet, she didn't let down her drawbridge
I asked her relentlessly, till I left her
My mute questions appealing to her
'My dearest, are you really happy?
Is this happiness real?'
She moved her head, nodding and shaking
Like a puppet, as if instructed.
On my way back, I comforted myself
'Look, she had to change, no more
Is she a baby, feeding on mash and milk
She is now a woman, the mistress of her house
A wife, a lover, and after all bound to her new life.
Didn't you bind her to the rules of her game
When you started her on her own game board?
Then why do you search her spoor
When she is following her game path?
When you taught her to walk on
Rose petal strewn paths, didn't you imagine
There would also be muddy tracks?
The fledgling has flown the nest
Why do you worry how it'll fly?

Some day her weak wings will strengthen
With great sky-soaring, is this
The time to clip her wings?
Hadn't she broken all ties with you
At your behest? Why do you want
To forge those bonds again?'

I scolded myself, broken and lonely
Again alone in my house
Thinking of her in an attempt to forget her
And then I saw light, the truth
She was now midstream, and I
Had finished my swim.
I now waded along the banks
While she revelled in the lave
I realized it was for me to
Watch her bloom from the side
Watch her soak and enjoy this lifestream
Emotion drenched, with her mate
My happiness in that she was swimming
Strongly, on her own, moving forward
My involvement only to lend a hand
From the banks, if she tired.
When she reposed on her luxurious bed
It was for me to hum to myself
The familiar notes of her childhood
So they would lull her, perhaps

If she sat basking in the tender
Rays of the gold sun on her terrace
It was for me to provide for protection, the shade
Of a parasol ready to be
Held out if the sun burned even a little,
A voice castigating, disapproving
Noting my interest, involvement
'Don't you know, the tree has to withdraw
Its shade, if the sapling has to grow;
You will stunt her with your extreme love
Haven't you played enough with her?
Let her have her share of life
Is she meant to be only for you?
When she stops hobbling on the crutches of your love
She'll find her bearings on the scented, grassy, soil.'

I looked around startled, it was
But my own mind, trapping me
In the dark corners of its dwelling, and warning
It was true, very true!
But hadn't I in the past been tricked in
These halls of the mayasabha* seeing limpid pools
Where they weren't any, wandering thirsty
As I was, with my doll in the enchanted forests
I had wandered till my feet cracked,
Enduring the amazement all with my doll clutched to my chest

---

* A palace built by the Pandavas to trick the Kauravas. It had highly reflective floors that were easily mistaken as the surface of a pool of still water and a pool of water with a surface that mimicked a floor, into which Duryodhana fell and was humiliated by Draupadi.

The terrible pain transmitting from my body,
My heart, to her, darkening her
As if bitten by a serpent
How can I let her be barefoot in that green?
She has to make her own way, I know
Through orchards, rocks, thorns and deserts
Of course, she will do that
But if I forewarn her, she will tread carefully
With the experience, and if wounded she must be
At least she will not be speared through.
I have withdrawn my shade in the past
To let her experience the warmth of the morning rays
Should I not then warn her of the intent of
The scorching, relentless heat of the sun at midday?
She has to take nourishment from this sun and grow
But can I let my tears mist my watch?
Her path has been lit by my vigil, but my eyes
Will be beacons, the nandadeeps* of navratri†
Carefully tended with wick and oil to spread the light
To guide her. The flickering flame that she is, needs
My gentle palms to steady her
She is now a shared responsibility, no longer solely mine
But I crave for just a word that assures, an act that assuages
A glance I can believe, some sign!
That she has been accepted, she belongs, is loved
I will slip away then, credulous of the trust
Content to watch from my hiding place, her growing,
Blossoming sunburst.
Until such time, I need to be on call, to be by her side

---

* A lamp that is kept burning ceaselessly, especially during navratri.

† Festival of nine nights.

With all my might, with my mate, any storm to bide
A target set, resolve made, insecure, unsure
I looked for support in the eyes of my mate and felt the
Gentle, calm waves from the ocean of affection
Lapping, soothing, comforting, placating
As I had always, when I fabricated my doll, when I wove
All those fantasies of her, for her, with my love and his
Then I realized that the journey we had traversed
Hands held, led and flanked by him seamlessly and silently
My worries and fears I reposed in him and
Dared to dream and hope again for my doll.

Sixteen

Her absence now a given, the house too humours me
Shadowing me silently as I wander through its sad emptiness
And I glean how the threshold had conspired to move
Ever so slightly, to avoid her unsteady baby steps
Letting me believe I had caught her stumbling.
My fervent pacing in the scent of her steps
Draws a mused response from the prajakta tree
Showering me with fragrant orange stemmed five-petals
It tells me to feel the silken touch of her tiny soles
On its moist and velvet white whorls.
When her memories swell through and
Madden me, the house indulges me and
Calms me with glimpses of her,
Leaning, swinging, sliding down the banister
Giggling, experimenting, cooking
Preening in front of the mirror
Hugging, jostling, laughing with my mate
The imp, sprite, mischief incarnate.
The house shows me this treasure, like a toy box
Again and again, with patience anew
But I feel this urge to see her and rush
To see her drenched with the dew
Of contentment, and with happiness flush.

Caught in this wheel of doubt
One day I felt a thistly prick
Like the beginnings of tarnish on the tinselled scales
Of the mermaid in the picture, like the fading colours
Of her once vibrant flesh, my doll seemed lustreless
Framed in her doorway, the auspicious designs
On the door frame still the same, not bearing semblance
To my doll, wan, listless, thin and unkempt
Hollow patient eyes, lips pursed in brave defeat
Hair askew, she looked at me askance
When I asked after her, "I will get them, mother, have a seat."

The welcome behind us, they did allow me to bring my doll home
To wash, to anoint, to love, to pamper, to indulge, to groom
I tucked her in her soft bed and crooned her to sleep
My touch a balm to her chaffed and cracked soul
I searched for the hints of her joy and sorrow
With every breath and sigh as she slept till the morrow
With great love I tried to inspire and instil confidence
Petrified, uncertain, she asks me hesitatingly
'Why did you give me away there?
I am unwanted, unloved, a parasite!
Just as I used to lure my friends to stay and play
You tricked them with the toys of my trousseau
Blinded by the lucre, they realized too late
That I came along with all the glitter on the plate
The gilt and trim of my gift board game
Beguiled them so, a lacklustre pawn that I am
I do not fit the frame.
Where do I fit, where can I be stowed

An unsightly tag, how can I be showed?
Even the household servants your gift allows
Have names and resumes to go home to
References to boast of, candidatures to show off
But how can I be boasted of, what antecedents to gloat about
Who am I, where am I from, of what family and clan
Not the name you gave me, but my real lineage span
How did they moor me, or did I get washed in
On gilded water? How long before the gloss wears thin!
Strange quandaries, answers stranger,
Beyond their limit, above their drift
Then they resort to what they know
Hide me, ignore me, also disown
I am brought out when no one is around
Myriad questions their eyes do hound
I am asked to testify to a crime not mine
I am thrown scraps of mercy as a favour
With scorn savage, their reputation to salvage
My anguished, punished, humiliated self to cover.'

Engaged in my own flight, my doll clutched to my breast
I stopped breathlessly, my heart hurting out of my chest
Fantasising about her happiness, I stepped on a burning ember
I asked her in my searing pain, 'But what about your playmate,
        my dearest
Does he join in, does he desert you, does he not love you?'

A sad smile crossed her sadder eyes

'My playmate is a mere marionette, cute,
Obedient, but nevertheless a puppet
He hasn't had the nurturing you gave me
He doesn't have the pride you instilled in me
He doesn't have the sense of self you inspired in me
He hasn't understood himself, so why should I
Quest after him? I am tired, beaten and wry
Little does he know I live in that house
So oblivious he is to my existence.
A lot of distance, some fear, some wonderment
A relationship is far away, distant, seemingly unattainable
Didn't I beg you to leave me at my lowly mortal level
My sensitivities, sensibilities, my expectations, my ambitions
Raised so high that no one can reach them
And if they do, no one can read them
What am I made of, he doesn't know!
And conceding me is beyond them
And loving me is beneath them
Enough now, don't push me away
At least till I rest my head in your lap
At least till I heal!'

Soundlessly I gathered her to myself
'Sleep my child, cradled in my arms
My efforts to see you happy in vain
Couldn't save you the disdain
I simply hadn't accounted for the stars conspiring
To make one's fate and future or upstage one's planning
And that name and patrimony were requisite, nay
Quintessential for the matrimony of offspring

Would I have sent you there, had I in my wildest nightmares
Foreseen your plight, hush, hush, my child, it's sad
That you found only old landmarks on the new path you tread,
Lingering unsightly vestiges, anomalies we dread
How can I console you, when I drown in commiseration?
Surely there is a spell to reverse this curse
Nothing can hurt us any more, can anything be worse?
Our irrational zeal to collect dewdrops in a sieve
Will help us support each other
Granted, the old game won't interest you much
But we'll play it afresh, with energy albeit forced
A strange game of three players, no winners, no losers
But only the promise that there will be no poking, prying,
No pain, the punishing pain
A promise made with the setting sun as a witness
A vow made with the dying light, to be kept
Till my dying breath.'

My doll relaxed, her fears dissipated,
Like a bird buffeted by gale and storm
Fluttering into the refuge of a crevice
Her heaving chest calming, her fear-widened eyes
Gently lowering their lids and lashes
To fan her cheeks, hugging her tight
A tree lacerated by the storm, my eyes shut unbeknownst
Tired and tearless, then why does a stray drop well up,
With closed eyes I ransack the recesses hidden within
Questioning, doubting, sceptical
'Will you consign her to a life bloomless?
Spring never did come to you, but can you see her

Condemned to a forced fruitless existence?
The cycle of seasons brings hope after despair
But to nurture a lonely sapling is beyond repair
Beware, all your efforts may go in vain
Your lives inane, a deep pain will remain.'

Seventeen

Now it's just the three of us in our bastion
Bound anew, but the days not halcyon
The pleasure of tasks quotidian
Tainted now by a dark shadow careworn
My mate, too soul-sick, a father failed
We count and count again, the days that remain
Knowing our memories alone will not sustain
Her vulnerable existence, when we are gone
The anxious, unsure worrying stays with as we sleep
And greets a new morn, the sunlight harsh in our eyes
Waiting in the knowledge that the warm rays
Will eventually blister the day, only to descend
At dusk, an emollient, to prepare for the morrow.

Propped up by our protecting arms, our fortress
Where the drapes of our love obscure the harsh glare
We scour our wounds at the end of each battle day
Only to wake to another fight, some more damning dismay
But my mate and I ever optimistic, believe this away
There will be a rose red dawn when the koel* will be the harbinger
     of spring
And the sun's rays will dance to melodies

---

* Asian cuckoo.

And will continue to shine after sundown
Like glow worms in the dark.
We need to let the searing pain subside
Then all will be well, our love shall abide.

Eighteen

Each passing equilateral day, stretched tight on our trio
Rejuvenates us for the next day's play
Blinkers on our eyes, side, fore and aft
We tread steadfastly, fixing the furrow
Beneath with laden lids and an anguished eye
Flanking our doll, we hold her upright
We three a string of beggars unsightly,
Moving on the board unexpectedly we sight
Strange feet, not unfamiliar, positioned to capture.
Stilled in our march, we unveil our blinds
Our eyes imploring, beseeching
'We moved her forth to your side in an erroneous move
But haven't we made right that wrong
With the least trouble and utmost care?
Why do you waylay us now, why this scare?
Or is it to destroy the last memory, the remnant
She may have secretly stashed, of her dare?
Forgive her, censure her not, for we swear
On our ancestors that never shall our paths cross
Nor will she ever transgress the board, we will prevent
Any move onto your side, neither square nor diagonal.
All her memories of the brief foray into your days
Obliterated for sure, pray put our stray encounter
Aside as unpremeditated, a mere accident.'

They listened, still blocking our move
As if they had to offer a gambit sound
Unstitching the materials of her mistakes
'Her moves rushed, rules broken, concentration flagging
A weak player and pawn, duffer that she is,
She seeks your signs on our side, engrossed in your game!'

I made a move, dared lock eyes with them,
Facing them with calm sincerity, posed my questions
'Is this the only reason for her banishment?
Was she not asked to account for her pedigree,
To enlist her kith and clan? I bequeathed her all of mine,
Yet you sought to source her ancestry!
Why wasn't she welcomed along with her history?
Why this digging at her, her roots, inextricably
Linked with mine? Weeded out of your game
I refreshed her mangled roots once again
Holding soil in my garden, green buds sprouting anew,
Your step trespasses my thorny picket,
But don't you know my reputation precedes me
For my doll's fearless, fiery, ferocious defence?'

A volcano, I was speaking my mind,
The embers stoked anew, my anguish a lava spew
I paused for breath and saw bewilderment
On faces that had been singed, too
In this fire play, little had they fathomed
The depth of the enchanted valley of flowers

Wandering after the wafts of perfumed allure
They unwittingly had trampled on the smouldering beds
Of the fire flowers they coveted
Treading after me, my footprints soiled
They believed it was but the dirt path,
Walking some more, they understood
My route was riddled with pitfalls
My journey unchanging and unending
The luxury of the grassy sides not mine
But they were lost, floundering, confounded,
And retracted their hesitant steps, disavowing,
But a tenacious thread unravelled thus far
From the rents and tears, a thread of hope,
Of human bondage, tugging at the memories
Of the game unfinished, the board abandoned
The thread giving them courage to appeal,
To seek for a sign, a precognition, a reprieve,
A second boon from the bountiful Mother Goddess!

My eyes felt their souls circumspectly
And took heart on the softness I touched upon
A desire, half formed roots of emotions
And the unravelled thread, hanging by itself…
Picking it up, I harnessed the loom, the warp and weft
Of my doll's future, an assiduous web to be woven
The fecund ashy soil ploughed, seeds of hope and dream sown,
Of happy vines climbing over her home in the sun.

I stepped back with the weight of possibilities
Delving deep into my heart, rending questions
'Is she welcome back? Will she be taken into your fold?'
An affirmation from their downcast eyes,
Triggers forgiveness too soon, a pardon too eager!

I know they are unsettled, plagued by a thousand
Insecurities, but I hang on to the tensile silken thread
Elastic, sticky. I design to sculpt out their affection, I steer them
Homeward bound with my doll, a second homecoming
Cajoling, encouraging, warning, even threatening
Firmly, I explain 'She is a part of you, to be cherished
Her pain you must bear, blanket her from fire,
I am beyond shame and fear, I am over the stigma
Another slip, a hint of suspicion, and her feet will spur
The path of return, irrevocably rolling itself up behind her
To my home, hers forever.'

The finality of my words, the resolution, firms their decision
And they return to their board, with my doll
Reposing on my shoulders the weight of their worries.

My repossessed doll goes back to her home
To restore her broken mirrors with resilience
And I look unblinkingly to store the last glimpse
Of her, wiping my tears with determination

And repeating to myself 'I will light
The path from my house to hers, day and night.'
My simple, meek and trusting doll lets herself
Be led like a lamb, on my say, my signal
Certain in the belief she will shored to safety
We bravely convince ourselves this is foreordained
Not our free will, nor a faux move trying to salve.

I pieced her out of threadbare castaway rags
Someone's trash, my treasure to design
I layered, darned, patched, sewed with pleasure
And then left her to her own,
Handfasted with the unacquainted, unknown
She quested to find a place, her place in the hearth
And home, finding it taken, usurped, searched again
Once more she returns to this game, her feet laden.
She will deal and spar and tire, her board her play will gladden
Then she will truly inherit my space, her secure corner
In my heart and abode, a haven to return to
A safety net, with me or after me
Until then, she must be in their gameplay
And try to find the safest corner,
And I remain from far hers, a watchful sentinel.
She mingles with them, awkward, unsure,
Trying to read nuances, between the lines
With every interplay, inconsequential or not
Their growing cognizance of each other
Bringing acceptance, perhaps inevitable
Yet they have grappled with question and concern

Infamy, disgrace, prestige, status, consanguinity,
Touched by stigma and rejection, societal and their own

Her birthparents' matrimonial status and predicament
Her astral signs removed like offensive graffiti
No longer a matter of perverse curiosity
Care and protection now winged over her
Affirmation that she may not require my spare corner.

The sun now rises and sets on time, stars shine
Winds blow, thunder and lightning strike
Seasons change as is their wont, and I watch
As the not-so-far-behind spring comes
To the mango blossoms in her garden
And my doll dancing with her mate
Their love coming to flower and to fruition.

Our knots slipping as theirs are tautening
A vacuum in me emptying my fears
Filling me with calm and contentment
I retreat from the scene of fulfilling love
Without tarrying, to my ever wakeful alcove.

Nineteen

Picking greens in my garden, my mate cautions
To spare the sprouting nodes and I assent
Loath to tear a leaf tender before its time
I select one ripe and ready, and hark!
I hear my doll's distinctive call, and I am bemused
Listen not to the pandering of my affection
Her call the rhythm of my heartbeat
Swinging my doll by the arms in play
I have started her spin but am no longer the centre of her gyre.
She has gathered her own speed, her rotation
Gives her an orientation, or will make her so dizzy
With happiness that she doesn't call out for me
My dogged mind I drag from the voice hearing,
Luxuriating in the proudly pregnant stem.
Immersed in its beauty, I stroke its softness,
When those cries I dismissed as my fancy
Crash on my ears like waves at high tide
Eager and bursting with excitement
And then the appearance most delightfully surprising
Like a sudden burst of a summer shower
Of the owner of the voice dearest, my beloved doll,
Radiant faced, flushed with happiness, a flowering vine
Our hearts beat in unison and I shut my flowing eyes tight
Framing her face like a delicate thought,

Her mere touch likens her to the stem I just cherished

My embrace still firm and tight I ask her hesitatingly
'My doll is this true? Really?'
A silent smile on her lips and a gentle touch by her
Just like mine on her head, comforting me
Squeezing her with joyous disbelief, I hold my breath
A miracle of the start of new life I witness
In the gilded red brilliance of the sunset at my door.
Morning flowers falling to ground by day end
Blossom-drop their blight, never reaching fulfilment,
This embryo of hope, strange to my barren bower,
Heralding the promise of a bounty of fruit
Ecstatic with joy unknown, running from idea to idea
I explored ways to pamper my expectant doll
Who brought glad tidings to my garden in fall
I chanced a glimpse of her looking at me
Observing the new me keenly, as never before
I held her hand, lacing her fingers with mine
Conveying my silent gratitude, for being loyal to
My affection and gracing my unprofitable tracts
With a gift so dear, confiding in me her rich secret
The barren tract trembles with frailty
And so do I with possibilities anew
I can't repay even for seven game sets nor forget
Her debt, her munificent endowment!

I lean over to search her lucid eyes, my grateful refrain

Echoing in her ears, she smiles, innocent and benevolent
Drawing the last shreds of curtains of pain and bitterness
She wants me to share in her newfound happiness
Frolicking with her in her new game
She shares how like a pearl in the oyster
The life inside her shapes and grows
'Now moving, now kicking, oh look
He's turning, heaving and scaring me
A part of me, inside me, yet he is the Other.'

She grows in meaning, more profound by the day
And I marvel as the chrysalis metamorphoses.

Wheat gold complexion, glorious hair a beauty bonus
My doll resplendent with the life growing within her
Content of countenance, party to the secret of life
Her full curves preparing to store the sap of life
She's full of meaning now, sumptuous and statuesque
I made her and she has far surpassed my reach!
Poised on the brink of motherhood, a state so primal
My doll, my dearly loved child becomes my mother.

I join her in this new game of waiting
Equally eager, excited, apprehensive,
At stages throughout my own game, I recall
We had felt so, nervous, had taken a step backward to fend,
Yet, I assure myself anew, hadn't we got a chance

To enter the game again after many a time-out?
What is the probability of a wrong dice throw?
Surely the master gamester isn't so inclement!

Twenty

A majestic sailing ship on a tranquil sea
She rolls gently towards a waiting harbour
Her senses intently aware of each fleeting movement
Of the vivacious life kicking inside her belly
My mate and I follow every movement in her wake.

Watching keenly, alive to every movement slight
Discerning every nuance of her breath or sigh we watch
With undivided attention day and night, alert and ready,
Preparing eagerly to welcome the advent
She grows slow, quiet, heavier with meaning
Abstracted, looking inward, soul-searching,
Listening keenly, expectantly to her heart
About to experience the emergence of a complete life
Created out of her, cording itself free gradually.
She searches an image of a self she senses exists
Not the deceptive mirrored reflection, a mere delusion
A groundswell of expectation surging through her
She gladly sports symptoms of her significant situation
Impatient to see the new player in the game
Yet smitten by the fear of the unknown.

The fear snakes to me as well, striking its whiplash tail
But I fortify myself to face its rearing head, its locking eyes
While pleading earnestly with the master for a square
Of rest, relief, respite
'You did not deprive her of a doll of her own
But even as you did so, will you take away
My adored doll to punish me for my audacity?
I would relinquish all my lust for life and game
If it meant she got a lease anew, a game continued.'

My pleas a heartburst, I contain myself
And tend to her, now fatigued with her weight
As if telling me albeit silently, 'Yes, the moment has come'
And it does, as suddenly! Wringing her body in pain
A wave rising and subsiding, carrying us all closer to it
The perfect storm continues, at times drowning
At once lifting, I watch her tossed like driftwood
In the troughs and crests and I rush to buoy her.
I give her courage, 'My dearest, this agony has an end
In the parrot green base of the tender new shoot.'
She smiles trustingly, through the excruciating pain

A gathering of others around her now, comforting
Supporting and sharing the anxiety around
Bound by a common goal, the celebration of nativity
A primal ritual, they prepare to welcome the newborn
And then the decisive seismic wave
That she bore down on, sweat-drenched

Her hand reaching out for mine.

Like a new shoot breaking out with life force
From under the sun-baked ground, facing the blue sky
A new form of life is separated from her
Delivered by the rogue wave into eagerly waiting hands
All heaving stops and then, the descending calm.

My dear doll, a fragile banana plant racked and lashed
By the storm, a state not unknown to her all her knowing life!
Gently mopping her beaded brow, I kiss her tenderly
Trying to suck out as much of her fatigue
Patting and stroking her, comforting her
My endearing, enduring doll smiles, deeply content
As my tears roll down her cheeks.
I watch her enlightened and serene face, a state
Never witnessed before, bewildered and confused.

'Where is he? My doll, my gift from the Maker?'
She asks, in a voice mellow with a new ripeness
Oh yes, where is he? My heart lurching
I remember him now, like a gift not unwrapped
Rushing to hold him, I bring him to her,
My doll's gift from the Maker, her very own doll!
I hold him close and inspect his perfection
He is without any defect, blame or blemish
Not a rag doll, nor fashioned from castoffs

By forlorn, disappointed hands, he is picture perfect
A cherub most pretty and innocent.
So flawless and fragile, I am wary of scarring
Him with the lines and ridges on my palms
I place him in her arms to snuggle cosily, rightfully.
She observes him, rapt, her doll, her very own
A natural, unconditional and unconstrained gift
From the Maker, hers forever.

She rises to cuddle him, a piece of her own flesh and life
And as if making a vow, she speaks solemnly,
'Look at him, my baby doll, a gift most blessed
I nurtured him within me, bore him and the pain
Inevitable and gave birth to him at the destined hour
That makes him mine, and I…I am his mother
But a revelation most meaningful I have experienced,
While I followed my destiny and obediently
Got played, you laboured with fortitude
The affliction, pain, suffering, albeit different,
But of the same intensity and magnitude,
In your venturesome pursuit of making me!
Without you and your audacious exert I would not exist
And neither would my baby doll, to rejoice
In this wondrous moment, the miraculous phenomenon!
I found my deliverance, but you are still stumbling
On with your pilgrimage to discharge my obligation.
His birth has revealed to me the extent
Of your lifelong torment, in respect and
Remembrance of which and in full cognisance
I reach out, call out to you, Mother!

Mother… my Mother… Mother…"

The stellar spectacle, of my doll, herself a mother
Dazzles me and I soak in the meteor shower of stardust
Lavished by the flood of her love, quenched, like her.

Unhooking the safety rope I entrust it to her
Secure in the knowledge that the other end of the cord
Will be anchored firmly by her baby.
My destination suddenly here, I am free
To bid farewell to her, along with my mate
An aura of our wishes good and blessings
Will always surround them all, my doll
Her mate and her very own baby, a gentle spirit
Guiding their journey into happiness and I
Will unwaveringly erase all the paths leading to her
As she embarks unswervingly, purposefully
On the way to her destination, the move to win her game
Supported and loved by her mate and her child.